SONIC PEACE

POEMS BY
KIRIU MINASHITA

TRANSLATED FROM THE JAPANESE BY
ERIC E. HYETT AND SPENCER THURLOW

PHONEME
MEDIA

Phoneme Media
P.O. BOX 411272
Los Angeles, CA 90041

ISBN: 9781944700409

Cover design by Jaya Nicely
Phoneme logo by Pablo Marín

Phoneme Media is a nonprofit publishing and film production house,
a fiscally sponsored project of Pen Center USA, dedicated to disseminating
and promoting literature in translation through books and film.

http://phonememedia.org

Curious books for curious people.

SONIC
PEACE

CONTENTS

PHASE 1: LIFE HISTORICAL PARADE

Lightbulb Bodies   **2**
Life History   **8**
The Sunshine Meter   **14**
Vending Machine At 4 A.M.   **18**
A-symmetry   **20**
March Road   **24**
Marginal   **28**

PHASE 2: PLASTIC CARGO CULT

Coelacanth Weather   **34**
Goldfish Friday   **38**
Water Falling   **42**
Intermezzo   **48**
The Name   **52**
Crowsong   **56**
Seventh Siren   **60**
August 31st   **62**

PHASE 3: HYPERSONIC STORYTELLER

Sonic Peace   **68**
Rhythm   **72**
Humid in Tokyo   **76**
Trio   **80**
Festival Of Water   **84**
Sunwater   **88**
Marginal/Eternal   **94**

Afterword   **101**
Note from the Translators   **103**
Translators' Acknowledgements   **109**
Author Bios   **110**

PHASE 1: LIFE HISTORICAL PARADE

電球体

電線の先で分裂していく
キョウノテンキの裂け目を縫い
こつこつと電球は点る
点在する思想のように明るみは閃く

晴れやかに沸騰する青い闇の中
とつとつと吐き出される食事風景のように

ツキアカリ　は　いつも
私の背中を射抜いていく

今日もケイタイデンワで
みんな
虫になっていく
虫になってみる
虫の思想の羽音が
青い闇の沸点を突き抜け

「言葉が電磁波とともにフルエルノダ」

世界がカオモジで記載される夜に
私は君とどの地点で待ち合わせよう?

シイピイユウシュウハスウ速度よりも速く流れる
このナニヤラネンチャクシツノヨウナモノを
どの時点で説明しよう?

Lightbulb Bodies

I'm splitting the end of the wire,
patching a tear in to· day's wea· ther
a lightbulb that's constantly
flashing like a bright idea.

There's always the moon— land· scape of
groaning thrown-up food

the blue darkness vividly boils around.
Everything's plugged in to my back—

these days, everyone
on their smart· phones
seeing what it's like to be a fly
turning into flies
the wing-sound of insect thoughts
roiling the blue-darkness.

"Words trem· ble with electromagnetic waves."

Where shall we meet, you and I, at night
when our world is described in emoticons?

That stic· k y some· thing
flowing fast· er than fre· quen· cy—
How can I explain?

君の手にしたクリティークと
私の手にした温度計の数値は
どの基点で対話しよう？

（ナゼナラ世界ハ　アシタ終了スルカモシレナイ）
（ナゼナラ私ハ　アシタ消失スレカモシレナイ）

日付が変わり
君の電球が点モル
私はそこを目指すのを止め

振り返ると

世界が反転していく
セカイガハンテンし、　テイク
文字のあいだを言葉が反転していく
そして鮮やかに回転していく
音と意味とガ回転シテイク

ソノ刹那
コノ瞬間ダケ可能ニナル
入レ替ワル
私ハ君ニナル
一瞬ダケ、君ニナル
気ヅカレヌヨウ君ニナル

シカシすぐニ
再び入れ替わる
今度私は小さクナル
猫の舌ほどに小さくなる

In your palm, a critique.
In mine, temperature.
How shall we interact?

(be· cause I can't know if   the world will end to· mor· row)
(be· cause I can't know if   I'll disappear to· mor· row)

It's a new day.
Your light bulb is on.
I've given up on that.

In the rear view,

the world is turning backwards.
The world   is turn· ing back· wards.
The spaces between letters and words are turning backwards.
Sound and meaning are revolving.
Then, vividly re· vol· ving.

For an in· stant
an only-now chance
to switch pla· ces
I be· come you
just for a second
become you, un· con· scious· ly.

But then
we switch back.
This time I become small, be· come
small as a cat's tongue.

見られないように
君を見る
気配を殺シ

アルカリ単四乾電池よりも細クナッテ
こっそり、君を見ている

Hidden from sight,
I'm watching you
kill the signs.

I'll make myself small· er than a triple-A battery
and keep watching you.

ライフ・ヒストリー

私が生まれたのはデボン紀の海岸
見上げれば赤紫色の空

私が持っていたのは四枚の鰭
未踏の水辺を不格好に移動する生

私が生まれたのは一〇四七階の産院
見下ろせば八五五階の工事現場

私が持っていたのは三本の腕に十八本の指
電気プラグの真下で音楽装置を操作する生

私は生まれた
原生音の鳴り響く浜辺に
太陽が接岸する朝に
プレ・大洪水地質学時代に

私が生まれた
金属質音声が調整する部屋に
防音ガラスが周界を遮る夜に
ポスト・神殺し地政学時代に

私が
生まれた
のは
先カンブリア時代の海中
透明な身体を
ふるふると揺らす生

Life History

I was born on the shores of the Devonian period,
above me the red-purple sky.

I had four fins
raw like a waterfront unwalked.

I was born on the maternity floor, ten four seven
looking eight five five stories down, a construction site.

I had three arms and eighteen fingers,
and an electric plug for operating live musical devices.

I was born
where the beach rings with a primeval sound,
the sun pulling alongside morning
the Pre-Deluge Geological Age.

I was born at night
in a room adjusted by a metallic voice
inside a perimeter of soundproof glass
the Post-Deicide Geopolitical Age.

I
was
born
in the Precambrian Sea
My transparent body
wiggling raw

私は
生まれた
のだ
オプティック・ファイバーで
遠隔操作される
試験管−内−生

私は、配視する

わたしがうまれたのは
にほんこくかながわけんべっどたうん
こうがいがたしんこうじゅうたくち
ぽすと
こうどせいちょうき
りょうさんがたかぞく
ぜんそくとあとぴーのどうきゅうせい
こりつしょうがっこう
こりつちゅうがっこう
こうりつこうとうがっこう

私は生まれた
大量生産された希望と
大量生産された生活史と
大量廃棄された死体の上に

私が生まれた
ディアスポラ・サイエンス時代に
ディスプレイ・パノプティコン
デジタル形而上学時代に
ＤＮＡ倫理学時代に

I
was
born remote
controlled,
fiber optic
Test Quality- Inner- Alive Within

I declare I

was born
Country of Japan / Kanagawa Prefecture
Another Et Cetera Town /
Suburban Subdivision /
Post-Advanced-Adult Age
Mass-produced type family
classmates with asthma and eczema
public elementary school
public middle school
public high school.

I was born
with mass-produced hopes
a mass-produced life story
dumped over a mass of dead bodies

I was born
in the eon of diaspora science
in the era of the panopticon
in the period of digital metaphysics
in the age of DNA ethics

私は生まれた

とりたてて　これといって
特徴のない、生
私　は

I was born,

in summary, all told,
alive. Nothing special,
me.

ヒナタ計

七月空の素白（ましろ）
あかるみに浸り
醸成していく明日の天気が
私の額で鳴り響く

太陽の線と圧力

日向計測器の目盛りが振り切れる刹那
夕陽は残虐に私を切る

八月透明自動ドアの直前
カタカナ機械軸の回転
背中に貼られた私の値札が
赤茶けた闇にヒルガエる

基点と角度

すだれのように揺れる空表面の下
発狂寸前なピュシスの二次加工物たちが歩く

歪んだセールス声と
暴徒のような救急車のサイレンが
この封鎖視界のはるか上から

だらん

とぶらさがっている

The Sunshine Meter

July sky's (true) white
steeped in shine
tomorrow's brewing storm
booming in my forehead.

Lines and pressure of the sun.

Sunset cuts me cruelly
as soon as the sunshine meter stops vibrating.

The price tag affixed to my back
flutters in the rusty darkness
in front of an August transparent automatic door
with a lettered rotating mechanism.

The origins and angles.

The sky's surface swaying like a bamboo blind—
nature remanufactured at the brink of madness.

Distortion—sales voices like
insurgents, ambulance sirens
far above this obstructed view

I swing

carefree.

私は
本の内部で溺れる紙魚のようなものになって
両目を凝らして計測する

計っているのに計られていく
読んでいるのに読まれていく
食べているのに、食べられていく

ヒナタの色　その真下
じりじりした接点の移動過程

思索ではなくコキュウされる意識の水面下
浮かび上がりを模索する気泡から
こぼれる甘味記憶を吸い尽くして
新聞紙の上は羽蟻がたかる

そして今日も
ドラム缶一杯の救済を求めて難民は歩く

記憶と疲弊の間に結ばれた平和協定のもと
空の素白のあかるみに浸り
忘音の場所　約束の時刻

君を待つ
美しき日に鉄屑が降る
美しき日が計られていく
美しき日に、計られていく

I'm something
like a silverfish drowning in a book.
straining both eyes to measure.

I measure though I'm measured
I read though I'm read
I eat, though I'm eaten.

A burning progression of touch
beneath the colors of sunshine.

A mooching flying ant
sucks underwater consciousness
from the newspaper,
sweet memory rising to the surface.

And today,
refugees walk in search of a drum can of relief

A peace agreement between memory and fatigue,
drenched in the brightness of sky's (true) white.
Place of lost sound   Time of accord

I wait for you
on a beautiful day of scrap iron rain,
a beautiful day being measured,
a beautiful day, measuring me.

午前四時の自動販売機

午前四時の自動販売機は
路上の水族館
電信柱の一個電球は
溜め息一歩手前
アスファルト上の影は
青くて長い螺旋階段

移行

始発の電車の音は
なぜだか不器用に響く
踏み切りの警報音は
空気中の唯一の固形物
道路上の缶カラと吸い殻は
絶対値零(ゼロ)

反転

変化の空と同化の空気は
そのまま一面の魚の群れ
停止と静止と中止の中間点で
看板は爆破一秒前
ブロック塀
乾燥したまま保存された博物館(ムゼアム)

音(リン)

Vending Machine At 4 A.M.

The 4 a.m. vending machine
is an aquarium in the street
the telephone pole's one bulb
sighs one step ahead of here.
Shadows on asphalt
a blue and long spiral staircase.

Forward

The sound of the first train
arrives awkward
the sound at the crossing
is the only solid thing in air
the hollow cans and cigarette butts in the street
are absolute (zero).

Reverse

Changing sky accommodating air
one side of a school of fish.
At the midpoint stopping halting pausing
the display about to explode
the block wall
the dried and preserved museum.

Sound (ding)

非－対称 <ruby>アーシンメトリー</ruby>

言葉が明滅する場所で
マドレーヌ・ヴィオネの旋律を聴きながら

私ノコトバハ
君ニ読マレルタビニ
言葉ニナッテイク

おそらく
バイアスカット・ドレスと
肉体が出会う時点のように
私　は
読まれなければならない

なぜなら
この空気密度の薄さの中では
かつての不在が
今では非在なのだから

世界が断片化する夜に
(夜ニ断片化スル世界ハ)
私と非－対称な欲望がバラまかれていく
(欲望ノ非－対称ナ私ヲばらマイテイク)

ココニアルモノハココニアルハズガナク
ここにあるものをここにながめながら

延々とエオスの登場を待つ

A-symmetry

In a place where words flicker
Madeleine Vionnet's melody is heard.

My words
be· come words
as they're un· der· stood by you—

most likely,
the way a bias-cut dress
fits the body,
is the way
I must be read.

Because
of the air's thin density,
the past
is nonexistent.

By night the world is fragmented
(the world frag· ments by night)
my asymmetrical desires scatter
(I'm scat· tered by my a· sym· met· ri· ccal desire)

Waiting endlessly for Eos to make her entrance.
There are things here that shouldn't be,

I'm look· ing at the things that are.

たとえば
立ち並ぶ
看板のネオンサインのように

たとえば
孤立する
駐車禁止標識のように

たとえば
組み換えられる
遺伝子情報のように

たとえば
移植される
人体臓器のように

たとえば
タトエラレナイケレドモ

この先の地軸を支え
夜更けの路上に立ちのぼる
君の
長い長い蒸気のように

For instance, how
neon signs
line up.

For instance, how
No Parking signs
stand alone.

For instance,
how genes
are recombined.

For instance,
how organs
get transplanted.

For instance,
there is no in· stance

like how the future earth will be supported
on its axis by you, standing, rising,
long, long in the late-night street
like steam.

三月道

呼吸を殺して雨が降る
路上のぬかるみの先
ニセモノの地平の上には
燦然と
シュミット＝ロットルフの青が輝いている

あそこから先は戦場なのだ
そう思い
近づいていくと
そこにはただ、陽の線

水の中
線の交点
君の分を空けて立つ

呼吸の狭間に雨が降る
線状に展開する空気の裂け目
トオイカチカイカハ意咲 ‒ を ‒ もたない
私はここで　君と話そう

眠り過ぎた朝と
三月は良く似ている
頭痛も似ている
硝子窓を汚していく
サンセイ雨も似ている
君の展開する

March Road

The rain spoils breathing
above the coun· ter· feit horizon,
where the muddy road
is ablaze
with Shchmidt-Rottulf's blue.

It's a battlefield,
from there on, I think,
but as I get closer,
just there, the sun's rays

intersecting
in the water,
separating your part.

Rain falls between breaths
in the linear slits of air
near and far have—no—mean· ing
Let's talk   right here.

March is overslept
like mornings
like headaches
like the a· cid rain
marring the glass window
that opens you.

徴分音　音　楽
<ruby>ミクロトーン・ミュージック</ruby>
のような言葉も似ている

発声練習にも似た郵便局員の声
発情する猫の声
発育過多な幼児の泣き声

すべては、雨の間に点在している

地を吸い
私は吸い上げ
ヤガテヤワラカク呼吸を止めて　雨が降る

架空の　「青の歴史」と
ミッキーミマウス・イリュージョン

アカルサノ強度コソガ環境ナノダ
（ウンヴェルト）
テレビモニタアから
目を背けてはいけない

目を背けてはいけない?

変化するキオンを飲み込み
呼吸を殺し

ひどく普通の顔をして
三月道を歩く
ひどく普通のしぐさで
三月雨を見る
ひどく普通の顔のまま
終了の音を聴く

26

March is words
like "microtonal music,"

voices of postal workers like choir practice,
voices of mating cats,
voice of an overgrown baby,

everything dotted with rain.

The rain sucks earth
I suck up the rain
that falls soft· ly,   stopping breathing,

The fictitious "History of Blue" and
Mickey Mouse illusions.

Each le· vel of bright· ness is an *Umwelt*.
I can't look away
from the TV monitor.

Can't I?

I swallow the changing tem· per· a· ture
killing breath.

I walk the March road
with a dreadful ordinary face.
I watch the March rain
with a dreadful ordinary gesture.
I listen to the sound of the end
with my dreadful ordinary face.

マージナル

明け方
かすかに地上をただよう残像を掻き分け

私の回路には　毎日
君の記憶が循環していく

いましがた
熱を飲んだばかりの風が
ジェット・エンジンに溶かされ

サウンド・バリア
障 − 壁の直前

周縁を描く場所では
風景の強度の内部に

ひそひそと

数値化されたての異郷が舞う

凶暴な人垣と　断続的な雑 − 音
音韻を聴く痛みを　じくじくとはらみ

コードレス / エンドレスな会話ノ波

君のいた場所
君のいル地点

誤差はいつも未来を志向し
ノスタルジア
未来は 郷 愁 を追尾スル

Marginal

At dawn,
an image pushes faintly through the ground.

Through my circuits every day
your data circulates.

Just now,
the wind drinks heat
melted by jet engines

approaching the sound barrier.

At that place, I draw the inner perimeter,
the strength of the landscape.

With a whisper

the strange digitized land dances:

intermittent noise of a violent mob
oozily swollen with the pain of phonemes.

Waves of cordless / endless conversations

the place where you were
the point where you are.

Errors are always the future
the future is always nos• tal• gia

見えるだろうか?

下層の温度差　上空の音階
境界線が投下される地点では
線而下に、だだ広い世界が伸ビる

ビー玉状に固まる視界を切リ取リ
振リ下ろされるボーリング作業の合間
内部に拡散されていく破片風景を痛む

周縁世界が溶ける場所で
開始と終止の二重奏を、痛む

can you see it?

The warm under-layers   the sky's upper scale
the points where boundaries are dropped
and below that surface, a fairly wide world.

The view is cut into hardened marbles
by a drilling rig swung down.
I feel the wasteland's inner pain,

at that place, the peripheral world dissolves
into beginnings and endings, a painful duet.

PHASE 2: PLASTIC CARGO CULT

シーラカンス日和

アキハバラ裏通りには
プラスチック製の言葉を
売っている店があるのです

今日見た商品は
ビリエ・ド・リラダン
の次に
ピリジン

窒素一原子もつ六員芳香族素環化合物
特異臭のある無色の液体
融点マイナス四一・八度
沸点一一五・五度
吸湿性　塩基性

それから棚を見回すと
シラー
の次に
シーラカンス

硬骨魚綱総鰭亜綱シーラカンス目の総称
白亜紀に絶滅したと信じられていたが
一九三八年、　南アフリカの南東海域で
現生種ラチメリア・カルムナエが発見された
全長約一・五メートル
対鰭は扇形をなす

Coelacanth Weather

In an alley in Akihabara
there's a shop where they sell
words made of plastic.

The first word I saw today,
(on the shelf above "Villiers
de l'Isle-Adam")
was "pyridine:"

An aromatic 6-part compound ring with one nitrogen atom.
Liquid having a distinctive odor.
Melting point: minus forty one point eight degrees.
Boiling point: one hundred fifteen point five degrees.
Absorbent.   Alkaline.

I look again at the display shelf.
right across from
 "Shiller"
is "coelacanth:"

Generic name for a bony fish, superclass osteicthyes, subclass
     coelacanthiformes,
believed to have gone extinct in the Cretaceous period.
Modern species, *Latimeria chalumnae*, discovered in 1938
in the waters southeast of South Africa.
About one point five meters in total
with paired, fan-shaped fins.

見上げると
コンクリート天井を突き破り
今日は素敵なシーラカンス日和

これ下さい、と
大声で注文すると

ああ、それね
展示品一点限りですが
よろしいですか
次回入荷の予定は未定です

と　オニイサンが
欠伸をつつ言うのです

I look up
through a crack in the concrete ceiling.
It's fine coelacanth weather today.

"This one please,"
I order in a loud voice

"Ah, that one—
It's the last. The display model.
Is that all right?
I don't know when we'll be getting any more,"

the man says
while yawn· ing.

金魚日

今日は金魚日だから
社員はみんな
ハンコを持って
社長室の前に
並ばなければならない

私の前に並んでいた
営業部のタカハシさんは
丸くて大きなガラス鉢に
素敵に立派な
赤いランチュウを入れてもらい
鼻高々で
社長室から出てきた

「お先に」
と言って
片手でネクタイをひねり
スキップしそうな足取りで
帰宅するタカハシさんを
社員はみんな
羨望のまなざしで見送った

まもなく
「次、入りたまえ」
と　社長の嗄れ声 がして
私がぎくしゃく部屋に入ると
社長は老眼鏡をかけ
秘書から渡された業績書を
ちらり
と一瞥し

Goldfish Friday

Since today is Goldfish Friday,
all employees are required
to bring their per· son· al· ized signature stamps
and line up
outside the President's office.

Mr. Ta· ka· ha· shi, from Sales,
who was in line, in front of me
emerged triumphant
from the President's office
holding a splendid, handsome
red Lionchu goldfish
in a large, round, glass bowl.

"Have a pleasant weekend,"
Mr. Takahashi said, and went home,
skipping gaily, and with his free hand
untwisting his necktie.
All employees saw
him off with envy
in their eyes.

"Next."
the President called out
in his gruff voice.
Awkward, I went in.
He was wearing reading glasses.
His secretary handed him
an employee evaluation form.
He glanced at it only once.

「ああ、君
君は、これ」
と　私に手渡したのは

ビニール袋に入った
黒い
ちっぽけな
デメキンであった

"Ah, you.
this one's you—"
and handed me

a thin plastic bag
with a tiny, black,
popeyed goldfish
inside.

落下水

良くできた
仕掛けオルゴールのような
乳母車の中の赤ん坊でした
私は強めの風邪薬のせいで
ちらちらする目をこらして　　（こすって）
見ていたのですが

やはり
それは水でした

幾本もの
細い
虹色に輝く水が
赤ん坊の身体から
吹き上げていたのです

私は必死 にそれを拭こうと
ハンケチでぬぐうのですが
水は
あとからあとから
さあさあと
吹き上げて来るのです

赤ん坊は
命の限りに
笑っていました
笑うと

Water Falling

It was a proper baby,
like a gimmicky music box
in its baby carriage.
I was high on strong cold medicine,
looking through
elaborate fluttering eyes (rub).

Anyway,
it was water.

Real-thing water—
water shining
a thin rainbow
coughed upward
by the baby.

I tried desperately
to wipe it up,
but I only had a handkerchief.
The water
came sputtering back down
again and again.

The baby was laughing
within the boundaries
of life.
The baby laughed,

いよいよ
水は
高らかに吹き上がりました

あ

大変だ
あまり水を流すと
きっと
死んでしまうのだ
どうすれば良いのだろうか

私は脂汗を流して
それを見ていました
しかし
誰一人
訝しがる人もありません

私は途方に暮れ
虹色に輝く
水の浸ったハンケチを握りしめ
ふと
振り返ると

路上は

しゅうしゅうと
水を吹き上げる人たちで
溢れていました

and finally,
loudly,
coughed more water up.

Ah!

Danger!
Too much water flowing.
Surely
he'll die.
What to do?

I was watching,
sweating oil,
but
no one
seemed to care.

I was at a loss,
my handkerchief clenched with
water
shining rainbow.
I looked back

at the street

completely
full
of people spewing water,

誰もが
きらきらと　　（てらてらと）
光る水を幾筋も吹き流し
誇らしげに

靴音を響かせ
歩いていました

私は恐る恐る
ショーウインドウに
自分の顔を映して見たのですが
別段変わったところはありません
ほっとして横を向くと
私の頭の後ろ
盆の窪のあたりから

ちろちろと

細い水が
流れ落ちていました

everyone
twinkling (brilliantly)
bright water streaming, proud
into every muscle.

Footfalls resonating,
walking

hesitant,
my own face projected
in the display window.
Nothing much had changed.
Relieved, I turned sideways to look.
Water from the back of my head.
Water from the nape of my neck.

Thin,

flickering,
flowing downward.

間奏曲

水溶性の空に向け
鉄雨を浴びた街路樹が
ふつふつと生命を吐く　夜
君が、私の前を歩いている

流動性の地平を避け
金属臭を帯びた葉が
しうしうと空中を這う　中
君の肩先に、路面月が宿る

間奏曲
インテルメッシオ

私が、　聴いている

スクランブル交差点
上から底から背後からの
音-差

私たちは
たった今
走り去ったバスの
ガソリン臭
ただよう路上を
歩く者たちである

私たちは
急に降り止んだ
汚染雨の気配と
歩く君たちである

Intermezzo

You're walking in front of me,
the night   vomits life.
The tree-lined street draws iron rain
toward the water-soluble sky.

The streetcar moon dwells on your shoulder
shushing and crawling through sky.
Leaves tinged with metal odor
shelter the liquid horizon.

In ter mez zo

I'm   listening

to the scrambled crossings,
the differing sounds
from the top from the back from the side.

Just now
we are the
people who walk.
The gasoline fumes
from a bus driving away
drift through the streets.

We are the beloveds
gone walking at the sign
that acid rain has suddenly
stopped falling.

交点
君の蒸気が、　歴史線に突きたっている

沸点
君の吐息が、　雨の名残に溶けあっている

私は　呆然としたまま
呆然とした、まま

Crossroad,
you are steam in the face of history.

Boiling point,
your sigh melting down into a rain-relic.

I'm   amazed,
amazed still.

名前

朝のプラットホームに
ぽつん、と一つ
丸い名前が落ちている

これ、君のかい?
と隣人は聞く

私は返事に困り
いいえ、とも
はい、ともつかぬ返事で
微笑する

こんな大事なもの
落としちゃあいけない

隣人はそう言って
拾おうとするのだが
それは　くるくると反転するばかりで
決して拾われようとはしない

ひっくり返った名前の裏には
厳かな金色の刺繍文字

コレハ嘘デス

なんだ、嘘か
と　隣人たちは
冷ややかな安堵の溜め息を漏らし
さざ波のように
電車に乗りこんでいく

The Name

Morning on the train platform
someone has dropped a name,
lonely and round.

The man next to me asks
"Is this yours?"

Without
saying yes
or no,
I smile my reply.

"You shouldn't go around dropping
such important things," the man says.

I try to pick it up.
It just spins away
never to
be retrieved.

Embroidered in solemn gold
on the back of the overturned name:

This Is Un· true

A lie?
Passengers
ripple onto the train
with sighs
of cool relief.

私は再び表に返し
半分消えかけた文字を読む

コレガ嘘デス

私は笑いながら　それを
コートの内ポケットにしまいこみ
速やかに、逃亡するのだ

I return and read again
the lettering half erased

This Is Still Un·true

Laughing, I place it
in the inside pocket of my coat
escaping, quickly.

烏唄

食紅を溶かした空の内部には
がらがらと
烏がチェインを引くように
嘲笑と　勝ちどきの声を
ねじ込んでいく

あ、あ、あ、あ、
ああっは、あああは　ああああっは、と

ようやく呼吸を整えている
衰弱死間際の地面には
季節外れに　恋鳴きする猫の精神が
だらん
とぶら下がっている

うるがあ、うるぐる
なあるなあるなあるないうるゆいん、と

この場所で
私は　さっき
烏の声に驚いて
白く小さな木枠を
落としてしまった

Crowsong

In the red food-coloring sky
rattling crows
screw out the sounds
of ridicule
and victory, a chain pulling.

caw, caw, caw, caw,
caaaaw, caaaaaaw caaaaaaaw

Finally breathing
on the verge of death-by-weakening
where the cat's unseasonable
caterwauling spirit
swings carefree.

graow-urgull
mew mew mew nao-miyaow

Just now,
In this place
amazed by the crows' voices
I dropped
a small white wooden frame.

枠組み内部にあったはずの
カタカナ名義の私の名前は
永久落下の道を辿り
私の影と君の呼吸を
細く
長く
明るみと流浪の中に
引き延ばしていく

でもその刹那

鳥、　飛ぶ

My name was supposed to be written
in *katakana* letters on the inside of the frame.
Follow the road's endless falling,
through the light and wandering
my shadow and your breathing
stretched out
long
and thin.

But at that moment

crows, fly.

七番目のセイレーン

十一月降下速度ノマシタ
晴れやかな空白ニタチツクス
はたはたと漂白サレテイクテンキ
音楽装置を露出サセナガラ

ツェ、デ、エ、エフ
の、音

天蓋あるいは空
ゲ、ア

ソラノハズレ

君のいた机の先に
雲、長々と
七番目の、音

Seventh Siren

November's descending ve·lo·ci·ty
bleached in flapping wea· ther
uncovers audio e· quip· ment
still standing in radiant blank· ness

cé, dé, é, ef
of sound

canopy? or sky?
gé, a

Emp· ti· ness

The desk that was yours
Long, long clouds
The seventh   sound.

八月三十一日

雨が日にちの曲がり角
金バケツもって歩いていきます
八月本日　雨ざんざ
鉄錆びの匂い歩く浮きます

雨が世界の曲がり角
私の髪の毛ぼろぼろ鳴ります

ぼろぼろぞらぞら
ざくざんざ

八月きのうも　雨ざんざ
向かいの猫も金切声で窓枠に　窓枠に
小枝を結ぶ暇さえなく

にいにいにいにい
ぎいにいにい

八月日暮れの　雨ざんざ
お薬のような匂いがします
水喰いの鳥が柳の木の下
すまして歌を歌います

ひら
ひらひらひらひらひら
ひ

雨が世界を崩して行きます
雨が世界を壊して行きます

August 31st

At the turn of the day the rain
goes walking, holding a golden bucket.
August today: torrential rain.
The odor of iron rust float-walks.

At the turn of the world, the rain
makes my tattered hair cry out:

tatter-tatter zora-zora
torrent-torrent.

August yesterday: more torrential rain.
The neighbor's cat screeching from window frame
to window frame, no time to pray for hope:

mee mee mee mee
scree mew-weww.

August nightfall's torrential rain
smells medicinal.
Birds eat water under willow trees
full-throatedly singing:

coo-coo
oo-eek, oo-eek oo-eek
croon.

Rain is destroying the world.
Rain is breaking the world.

雨が世界の曲がり角
私の靴が悲鳴をあげます

ぎう
ぎうぎうぎうぎうぎうぎう

薄ぺらいゴム底の下
アスファルトのでこぼこ
でこぼこ　感じます

ぎうぎうぎうぎうぎうぎう

雨が私の曲がり角
錆びたバケツに集めております

八月　おしまい　雨ざんざ
八月　終わりの　雨帰り

At the turn of the world, the rain,
my shoes cry out:

gloop-glosh
gloop-glosh gloop-glosh gloop-glosh.

Beneath the floozy rubber soles
the unevenness of asphalt
I feel   uneven:

gloop-glosh gloop-glosh gloop-glosh gloop.

At the turn of myself, the rain
collects me in a rusty bucket

August	ends with	torrential rain
at the end	of August, the rain	returns home.

PHASE 3: HYPERSONIC STORYTELLER

音速平和

太陽の下で
交換可能な私の日常は
イラナイモノからできている

この場所を取り仕切るのは
熱膨張を繰り返す意志
おそらく現時点では
金属コードからできている

君の皮膚の下を循環するのは
淡水系ヒドラ実験のように
晴れやかな精神

意志の白が沸き上がる地点で
暴走する無拘束物質と抱き合い
文法に乗った私の思想は
よろよろと立ち上がる
（シカナイノダシカナイノダシカナイノダ）

生存スルモノハ
生存スルハズノナイモノ

私たちは
いつも
私たちに裏切られていく

太陽の下では
新しいものは何一つ成立せず
名前のついた私の日常は
呼ばれるたびに消えていく

Sonic Peace

Under the sun,
every day is replaceable
made of things I don't need.

Whatever is in charge here
is likely made of wire
and also, the repetition
of thermo-expansion.

Your immortal psyche,
like the freshwater hydra experiment,
circulates beneath skin.

I embrace the runaway substance
at the point where my will rises white
my thoughts
stagger on syntax—
(on• ly, on• ly, on• ly.)

Whatever survives
de• fi• nite• ly should not have survived.

We always
betray
one another.

Under the sun,
my everyday has a name.
Each time I call it, it disappears
without creating even one new thing.

私たちは
タタカイながら移動する
タタカイながら世界を歌い
タタカイナガラネムル
（しかないのだしかないのだしかし）

空の青が空け開く徴の真下で
クダラナイコトでできている
砂糖城の天辺から
手を振る私の視界を超え

やがて世界に越境雨が降る
音もなく
水分の匂いをまきながら

私が
太陽の下で拾い集めた養分を
くつくつと溶かし

地下水脈に呼ばれ
正午の時点に（ゲンザイの地点に）
音速の雨が降る
無条件降伏によく似た私の影を飲み干し
転調を繰り返す君の精神の頭上
高らかに　雨は舞う

We
move while fight· ing
sleep while fight· ing
sing the world while fight· ing
(only, only, but only—)

I wave to you from the top of our
su· gar-coat· ed trash castle,
an omen of the open blue sky
beyond my sight.

The smell of moisture is rolled up
into border-crossing rain that will soon fall
on the world without a sound.

I gently disperse
the nutrients I've picked up
under the sun.

At the stroke of high noon (at this par· ti· cu· lar place)
a sonic rain falls,
called to an underground water vein.
Your spirit changes key again,
and drinks my shadow's unconditional surrender.
Rain   dances loudly.

オンリツ

喧噪と私の耳朶を濡らし
混雑気味な日常の上に
しらしらと
ルクレティウスの原子の雨が降る
眠たい不協和音と
数滴の了解域を飲み込んで

恒常的な騒音と圧搾機の夢を越え
震える世界と傘の林が一面
ナノハナバタケののどかさ

小型犬が吠えたてる
小柄な女がそれを叩く
小粒の雨が髪に染み入る
小学校の校庭で
小声で誰かがハミングしている

聞き分けいるとそれら声には鮮やかな音律

君のた、、めいき
には
劇薬が混じっている

街角には多数の空気袋
浮かび
そして
呼吸するたび
信号機が腐っていく
みんなワになる
ここにあるのは赤錆ばかり

Rhythm

Lucretius's atomic rain
falls gradually
above daily congestion,
wetting my earlobes with noise.
I've swallowed the good parts of several drops
sleepy dissonance.

On one side, the trembling world, a forest of umbrellas.
Beyond dreams of homeostatic noise and air compressors,
a serene garden of flowers.

Little dog with a rising bark.
Little woman smacking it.
Little pellets of rain that stain into my hair
Little courtyard of an elementary school
Little voices humming

If you listen closely to those voices' noises, there's vivid rhythm.

Poison
is stirred
into your s-igh.

Several bags of air
float at the street corner.
Then,
the traffic signal rottens
with each breath.
What is here is only red rust,
and ev· ery· one gets a· long.

天空に向かって落下していく
今日の日付と
私の足下の
ため息を吐く石の間を
切断していく
凍れる飛行機雲の線上
姿勢を正す間もなく
ぬくぬくと日は暮れる

君が呼ぶ
大仰な所定動作の狭間
山脈を成す
ユニバーサル・ビルディングのふもと

見上げれば

冷ややかな明るい闇の真ん中で
呆然と耳を澄ます私を嗤い
貪欲に陽は溢れる

I sever
today's date
that falls toward heaven
from the spaces between the stones
that give sound to the sighing of my feet.
Soon, the day becomes dark
tidying up a snug
line of ice-contrails.

When you call,
I'm at the base of the Universal Building in Nakano
where I build a mountain range
in the exaggerated spaces of required etiquette.

I look up.

Right in the middle of a bright frozen darkness
the greedy overflowing sun
laughs at me, straining my ears, amazed.

東京水分

中央線の両端は
物語の開始と終焉を引き受けず
黙視したまま　午後の昼寝

電線とブロック塀の気泡を斜めに切断し
氷結雨は地面から湧き上がる

その間隙
今日も金属質の祝福を浴び
ヨウセキリツセンゴヒャクパーセント のビルが建つ

雲ホコロビからは
空の代わりに純正律の言葉が見える

虚空を塗りつぶすペインタア
インストール済みです
と物売りは言う
色相環六角形を片手に物売りはささやく

コンビニエンス・ストア前アゴラには
コンビニエンス・シツギョウシャたちが
集う　飲む　食べる　吸う　捨てる　笑顔

キイロイカンバンノ徴ノシタデ
ゴソウダンニノリマス
ゴリヨウハケイカクテキニ
とコマアシャル　笑顔

Humid In Tokyo

The first and last stops on the Chuo Line
are the beginning and ending of a story
I completely miss   while napping.

Furious freezing rain angles up from the ground,
cutting wires and cinder blocks diagonally.

The gap between buildings
zoned for ma· xi· mum per-floor den· si· ty
is bathed in metal blessings.

From the cloud-seam,
instead of sky, I see words in musical intervals.

A street vendor says
the painters who fill the Void
have finished their installation.
The vendor whispers, a hexagonal color wheel in one hand.

In the agora in front of the convenience store,
the conveniently   un· em· ployed
assemble   drink   eat   smoke   trash   smile.

Happy to oblige
the om· in· ous yel· low sign· board:
In· ten· ded For Com· mer· cial Use
smile.

詩ナンカ書イテイルヤツハミナイズレ
ダンボール箱ズマイダ
と君が言う　笑顔

世界は晴れている

晴れながら凍っている
かたかたと日向は震え
震えながら晴れわたる

晴れた午後の日溜まりには
祝宴と死亡記事とコンバンノオカズが
並記される
そして廃棄される

世界の 結末 は穏やかに訪れつづける
　　　カタストロフィ
穴の空いた道路に足をとられた瞬間に
私は世界の落日を見る

しかし　ソレラハ幻覚かもしれない
コレラモ幻聴かもしれない

すぐに転調する

秒速で音階は血液をめぐる
今日は八分の六拍子で

声がする

東京水分、いりませんかと物売りは言う
純粋音程間隔で、物売りは歌う

That guy living in a cardboard box
must be wri• ting some kind of un• seen poem,
you say,   smile.

The world is sunny.

Frozen and sunny,
the sun trembling and rattling.
Pleasantly sunny while trembling.

In a sunny spot on a sunny afternoon,
weddings, death notices, to• night's ap• pe• ti• zers
are lined up neatly,
then tossed.

The end-of-the-world catastrophe keeps coming gently.
Every time I step into a hole in the road,
I see the setting sun of the world.

Still, I can't tell if I'm seeing things,
or hear• ing things?

Right away, a change of key—

today, the beat correlated to my pulse
in 6/8 time.

I hear voices—

Tokyo Humidity For Sale, sing the vendors,
in perfect pitch.

重奏帯

燃料不足の夜に
ネエアカナイハコガアルノヨアケテ
と猫が鳴く
私は
ミミガオカシクナッタワタシ
を眺めながら独りでに歩く

君は幻でも見るように私に聞く
同じ構想物なのに
ドウシテコンナニチガウノダロウカ?
ウチュウハスベテ
オナジモノカラデキテイルノニ
ソウダネ
モクセイモキミモオナジザイリョウカラ
デキテイル
デ
デ
デ
デ
デ、キテイル

私はただ
がたん、と落ちる
缶コーヒー一本分の重みなのだろうか?

晴れた夜の周縁をなぞり
打ち上がられる自動販売機の点在灯は
キボウノシルシなのだろうか?

Trio

Tonight, the fuel's run out,
the cat's squealing:
There's a package for you! Open it! Open it!
I am
automatically walking while looking at myself—
my ears look so strange!

My sweet illusion, you ask me
why are we so diff• er• ent?
We're the same ba• sic con• cept—
Space is all
made of the same bull• shit, you say.
It's true.
Both you and I
are made of the sa-
sa-
sa-
sa-
sa-
same stuff as Mars.

How heavy, exactly,
is the can of coffee just dispensed?
Ka-chunk.

Flashing lights on the vending machine
chase around the perimeter. Nighttime,
isn't that your fa• vor• ite brand?

君は
いつかの昼間に
わたしと出会うのだろうか?

私は
こんこんと湧く白い日向に
きみが映し出されるの待つのだろうか?

しかしゲンジテンデハ
視界不良のヨルの内部 で
猫の波形和音が重奏帯を築き
君の髪を揺らしている

聴き解すように
その場所に手を伸ばすと
猫、鳴き止む

Wouldn't you
like to meet up with me sometime
during the day?

Am I just waiting
for you to be projected
out of gushing white daylight?

How· e· ver, at this point,
in the night's low visibility, the cat's
synthesized wailing completes the trio.
Your hair is swaying

like you understand—
when you reach for me,
the cat   shuts up.

水宴

キリサメは
アスファルトから吹き上がり
冷え冷えと視界を遮る

長々と
ネジられもちあがる
地（デアッタハズのモノ）の線

祭りの最中
（イントラ・フェストゥム）

私たちは
太陽光線の振動とともに
増殖をつづける

個体の偏差とパスカルの孤独

たとえば
ゾーエーのささやかな輪舞を黙視する
飢餓芸人のように

世界はいつも
明日終焉を迎える直前に静止し
轟音の中心できらめいている

またもや周縁を描き
乾燥したイチ日の蓄えを水浸して

ひなたに水か点り
君の歩行跡には水分が残っている

Festival Of Water

My view is blocked
by ice driz· zle
rising from asphalt.

The lines of (what should have been) earth
are endless,
twis· ted up.

At the feast (*intra festum*)

we keep quivering
with the sun's rays
like growing plants.

Pascal's human misery, on a personal day.

For example:
the way a hunger artist disregards
the round dance of life*—

At the heart of its roar,
the world is always sparkling
in the stillness before the end.

Flood the stores of de· sic· ca· ted days,
draw the boundary once more.

You leave behind a wet trail
lit by sunshine.

眺めれば

爛々と
世界は伸び広がっていく

熱の波　水の煙幕
終焉の夕方に世界は伸び広がっていく

しかしながら垂直に落ちていく
巨大な疑問符の影

日はただ白昼の宴の中終わるのだろうか?
それとも水煙の底に沈むのだろうか?

（オカシナコトニ）私の目前には
雨の形跡ではなく
水分が残っている

しくしくと道路の匂いをばらまく
あの雨ではなく
君の水分が、残っている

If I look

the world is glaring,
stretching and elongating.

In the end, the world is expanding:
wave of heat,   smokescreen of water.

But I'm interrupted by the shadow of a giant
question mark falling straight down.

Will the day end in a feast of broad daylight?
Or will it sink into spray?

(How biz• zare) right before my eyes,
I see wetness
that didn't fall as rain.

Not the water of the rain
that strews the road with sorrow.
But you,   left behind.

* translators note: Minashita uses the Greek work *zoe* to describe "bare life,"
a reference, we believe, to the concept developed by philosopher Giorgio Agamben.

ひなたみず

いつまでも乾かない
夏の路上にて、想うのです
そこでは
ぬかるんだまま　ぬかるんだまま
空気が
えんえんと水温をはらみ

どこまでも　どこまでも
泥と草とボオフラの卵の匂い
のする　ひなたみずが
つぷんつぷん　と
うすくさざ波をたてております

水たまりの表面に映る空は
ゆるく鈍く厚ぼたい
世界が冗談のように見えてまいります

風の音カンケツ

私は
ゆらゆらゆれる空気の波に
つかまらぬように
ぐらぐらまわる頭を必死に起こし
聴くのです

いつまでも
いつまで、も

ざりざりと太陽が
私の中を通過いたします

Sunwater

My thoughts
are muddy   muddy
on the summer
road forever wet—
the air eternally pregnant
with water and temperature

everywhere   everywhere
sunwater. Plinking ripples,
fine bubbles
that smell of mud   of
larva and grass.

The world looks like a joke,
the sky reflected in loose thick dirt
on the surface of a puddle.

Spo• ra• dic wind noise

I listen to the wave of air
that trembles without catching me
l listen—
my wobbly spinning head
wakes into desperation.

Forever
and also, ever,

the sun
grits through my center.

重うくぬかるんだこの地面の上にては
ああ　このように
世界は終わっていくのカモシレナイと
ぼんやり
夢想するのでありました

どこまでも　どこまでも
夏と水の戯れあう音が
つぷんつぷん　と
うすい障壁をめぐらす　最中

夏につかまれからみとられて私は
おだやかに　ひそやかに
狂っていくのでありました

いつまでも　いつまでも
泥と草とボオフラの卵の匂い
のする　ひなたみずが
つぷんつぷん　と
うすくさざ波をたてております

ひなたの匂い　ひなたの匂い
ひなたの匂い　ひなたの匂い

見上げれば　発火する一秒前の空

どこまでも　どこまでも
泥と草とボオフラの卵の匂い
のする　ひなたみずが
つぷんつぷん　と
うすくさざ波をたてております

As for the world, atop this
heavy, muddy ground: is it end· ing?
Ah,   like this
I was lost
in vague reverie.

Wherever   wherever
the sound of summer playing with water
builds a film of fine bubbles
in the midst of   now

Summer caught me, cared for me
I was going
softly crazy.

Everywhere   everywhere
sunwater. Plinking ripples,
fine bubbles
that smell of mud,   of
larva and grass,

fragrant sunlight   fragrant sunlight
fragrant sunlight   fragrant sunlight.

I look up   one second before the sky ignites

everywhere   everywhere
sunwater. Plinking ripples,
fine bubbles
that smell of mud,   of
larva and grass.

こうして　私は
この地面の上で

いつまでも

どこまでも

聴きつづけるのでありました

ひなたの匂い　ひなたの匂い
ひなたの匂い　ひなたの匂い

And so,
on this earth

forever

wherever

I kept listening—

fragrant sunlight   fragrant sunlight
fragrant sunlight   fragrant sunlight.

マージナル/エターナル

明け方
かすかに地上をただよう残像を搔き分け

私の回路には　毎日
君の記憶が循環していく

いましがた
熱を飲んだばかりの風が
ジェット・エンジンに溶かされ

障 − 壁の直前
<small>サウンド・バリア</small>

周縁を描く場所では
風景の強度の内部に

ひそひそと

数値化されたての異郷が舞う

凶暴な人垣と　断続的な雑-音
音韻を聴く痛みを　じくじくとはらみ

コードレス／エンドレスな会話ノ波

君のいた場所
君のいル地点

誤差はいつも未来を志向し
未来は 郷 愁 を追尾スル
<small>ノスタルジア</small>

Marginal/Eternal

At dawn,
an image pushes faintly through the ground.

Through my circuits   every day
your data circulates.

Just now,
the wind drinks heat
melted by jet engines

approaching the sound barrier.

At that place, I draw the inner perimeter,
the strength of the landscape.

With a whisper

the strange digitized land dances:

intermittent noise of a violent mob
oozily swollen with the pain of phonemes.

Waves of cordless / endless conversations

the place where you were
the point where you are.

Errors are always the future
the future is always nostalgia

見えるだろうか?

下層の温度差　上空の音階
境界線が投下される地点では
線而下に、だだ広い世界が伸ビる

ビー玉状に固まる視界を切リ取リ
振リ下ろされるボーリング作業の合間
内部に拡散されていく破片風景を痛む

周縁世界が溶ける場所で
開始と終止の二重奏を、痛む

明け方
かすかに地上をタダヨウ
凍れる　陽射しを　掻き分け

私のカイロニハ　毎日
君　ノ　キオク　が　循環していく
君の記憶が流れるトキ
たしかに　君を受容していく

明け方ひたひたと
地上をナガレル　交流線のように

私は
君ニナッテ
この風景　ソシテ
この拡散記憶を
呼吸していく
ドウキしていく

can you see it?

The warm under-layers,   the sky's upper scale,
the points where boundaries are dropped
and below that surface, a fairly wide world.

The view is cut into hardened marbles
by a drilling rig swung down.
I feel the wasteland's inner pain,

at that place, the peripheral world dissolves
into beginnings and endings, a painful duet.

At dawn
frozen sunlight pushes
through   the   ground.

Through my circuits   every day
your   data   cir· cu· lates.
Truly, I'm receiving you,
those me· mo· ries flow.

Dawn flows   like power lines
steady over the earth.

I become you
a landscape of you.
I syn· chro· nize,
breathe in
the vapors
of your memories.

君と交差する歴史軸の上で

たしかに何度も
かすかに　地上をただよう残像を掻き分け
君の回路には　毎日
私の記憶が循環していく

周縁世界が溶ける場所で

遠くに
現−在　　をのぞむ円環の最中

明　け方　に

We cross on the timeline

truly, so many times
pushing faintly   through the ground
through your circuits   every day
my data circulates.

The peripheral world dissolves

far away for now
into a circle   of hope

at   dawn—

AFTERWORD

"Things which are unnamed are much more terrifying than those with names". So said Kobo Abe (pulling from Thomas Mann). Before the lion was named, it was feared as an evil spirit and called a supernatural being. But once it was given the name "lion", its being was converted into the realm of simple nature, and thus changed into an animal that can be conquered by humans.

My interest is what is lost in this conversion. To be specific, at the moment when the generative force of nature is converted into a natural force that can be calculated. It is here that what is lost trickles out like an excess.

The struggle that exists in contemporary poetry as well as philosophy and literature over the meaning of what is "named" has an inherent lifeline in the question: what kind of lion is it anyway? When the majority of lions are bred in cages, does the soul (anima) dwell there? Certainly at first glance, this is the kind of thing that's likely to be considered "fake", "a sham" or "a simulacrum". However, the situation is not so simple. In current trends even the soul (because it's the soul) is being consumed. The borders between genuine and counterfeit have been blurred.

Things that are "irreplaceable," depending on their "irreplaceability" are given commercial value (and rapidly progress into obsolescence). Even while boasting of its rapid strength and speed, the world is being ecstatically eroded by the violent rewriting of meaning. At least, it looks that way to me.

In this context, the goal of this collection of poems was to accurately reflect the world's strength's and speeds. It is probably, in fact, almost certainly, a reckless attempt. I continue to offer my hope-- full of contradictions-- as a hope heavier than despair.

Kiriu Minashita
Tokyo, June 2005

NOTE FROM THE TRANSLATORS

(A version of this essay was originally published in *The Cincinnati Review*, July 2015)

The problem of translating Japanese poetry into English is the difference in writing systems— a problem worth facing in the work of Kiriu Minashita. On March 11, 2011, Miyuki Yokota Nouguchi, a translator who lives and works in Tokyo, was finishing the Japanese edition of Julia Child's memoir, My Life In France, when the Great East Japan Earthquake and Fukushima nuclear disaster struck. Miyuki called Eric Hyett, a friend since their student days in Tokyo in 1989. Together they began working closely together on Twitter, in the aftermath of the 3/11 disaster, to translate and ferry necessary data between nuclear scientists in Japan and the USA who felt they were being pressured by their institutions to withhold critical information.

During this extremely troubled period, Ms. Minashita published a poem called Cruel Spring in a Japanese newspaper, the Asahi Shimbun, in which she implicates, literally, everyone—people, water, the earth itself— in the events of 3/11. Miyuki knew Minashita (who also publishes under her given name, Rieko Tanaka—it is customary for Japanese poets to use a nom de plume) through literary circles and sent the poem to Eric, who helped put together a rough translation. It was easy enough to get the essential Japanese translated, but very difficult to make an English poem out of it. The project stalled for about a year until Spencer and Eric met in a Boston poetry workshop, and discovered a shared passion for Japanese. We loved Minashita's work, and located the only copy in the Boston area of her first book, Sonic Peace, at the Harvard-Yenching Library in Cambridge. We decided to work together to translate her poetry.

We feel a special obligation to Ms. Minashita, who has given her blessing to our translations. She is a well-known poet and sociology professor in Japan, a public figure who frequently appears on TV, and the winner of several prestigious awards. In addition to poetry, Minashita is known for extensive critical writings on literature, as well as numerous academic papers concerning topics such as health care ethics and welfare sociology, transformation of the body experience and consumption culture. She also teaches sociology at Rikkyo University.

Minashita's work is hard to categorize. She writes in informal Japanese, modulated by western poetic styles and forms. Technology is her central theme, the techno-landscape of Tokyo figures prominently in her poems, which are deeply critical. In bringing her work to life in English, we hope the reader will recognize Minashita's passion for language in fabulous layered metaphors, and a poet's concern for her country and its technological society, by which she feels the Japanese ethos is threatened in an existential way.

Minashita's work poses some unique challenges for the translator. She plays tricks with language that are next-to-impossible to replicate in English. Most distressing (to us) was her deliberately-ungrammatical use of katakana, a Japanese writing system normally reserved for words of foreign origin. Minashita's poems veer into katakana seemingly at random, sometimes mid-sentence, or even mid-word. The use of stylistic katakana is well-documented in classical Japanese poetry, and most translators (since the 1800's) have ultimately ignored it in the English versions. However, based on our conversations with Minashita, we learned that her intention with the stylistic katakana is to isolate sound from meaning. We considered many approaches, but finally settled on a dot, similar to that found in a standard dictionary to separate syllables.

Another concern is her use of extraneous spaces between words, which is (deliberately) ungrammatical in Japanese. She calls attention to spacing issues in her poem Lightbulb Bodies, where she writes:

the world is turn ing backwards.
The world   is turn· ing back· wards.
The spaces between letters and words are turning backwards.

Minashita's work is challenging, and getting it right was a very slow process. When Spencer moved to Japan in March, 2014, we shifted our twice-weekly meeting to video conferences, and used Google Drive so we can both look at and edit the same document simultaneously. First, Spencer would transcribe the poems into an online, shared document. Working from his apartment in Kochi city on the island of Shikoku, Spencer typed the poems line by line from a paper copy of Sonic Peace. Although commercial OCR software is available for Japanese, the manual transcription process increased our depth and understanding of Minashita's work.

After the poem was transcribed, we'd meet and create a word-for-word translation. In this draft, we focused on core meaning, and paid less attention to syntax or stylistic beauty. We spent time on critical analysis, discussing her images and themes. We also conducted our own research into subject matter. For example, in her poem Coelacanth Weather, she references Villiers de l'Isle-Adam, a 19th century French author, and also discusses the makeup of the chemical compound, pyridine. We had to study these subjects in order to accurately embrace Minashita's intention. Sometimes we made difficult tradeoffs: for instance, the fact that pyridine and Villiers de l'Isle-Adam appear in alphabetical order in Japanese is lost on our English reader-- the sounds for p and v in Japanese are alphabetically adjacent.

Next, we would re-write the rough draft with a version that we believe works poetically in English. In this draft, we'd correct for line order, sentence order and word choice, making the English syntax as appealing as possible, while also conveying Minashita's message. In almost every case, our line order is entirely different from the Japanese original. For instance, in a couplet from The Name, the literal word order within the couplet would translate as:

this yours?
the neighbor asks

In our version, we've reversed the line order and cleaned up the grammar:

The man next to me asks
"Is this yours?"

We did this to make the poem sound natural in English, which has a wholly different sentence order— in Japanese, the verb always comes last. Establishing this second draft often required several sessions, as well as research into the Chinese characters, kanji, used for

Japanese. We'd sometimes look at the classical Chinese equivalent for comparison of specific and related meanings.

After we were satisfied, Eric brought each poem to poetry workshop (at PoemWorks, in Boston), where it underwent a review by roughly a dozen American poets, sometimes twice. This was the most critical step in our process, where important readability issues were often addressed. By the end, Workshop members had gotten very good at understanding what could and could not be changed with respect to the underlying text— knowing that Japanese has no distinction between singular and plural, for example, or definite/indefinite articles. In the poem Lightbulb Bodies, the workshop suggested "a moon" should become "the moon". And "a landscape" should be "landscape." These changes are for the sake of sound and meter.

Workshop members also frequently commented "sounds too Japanese" whenever we'd forget to swap the line order, and so we learned from poets' feedback how to make Minashita's unique voice work in English. After revisions and a final edit for punctuation, (which Minashita uses only rarely, and which we use throughout for readability), the poem in English was complete. We repeated this process for each of the 23 poems in Sonic Peace.

Kiriu Minashita is not a traditional Japanese poet. In contrast with traditional forms like haiku and tanka, her poetry relies entirely on Western styles and free verse, with lines and stanzas of varying lengths. In this way, her work is more in dialogue with Western poets than with the Japanese masters, though she alludes to both Yeats and Basho with equal facility. While Minashita does pay close attention, at times, to rhyme and meter, she does not do so in a consistent way. This created a real challenge for us in laying out a bilingual edition.

Japanese books are read from right to left, with the text oriented vertically. Our initial attempt to lay out the poems using vertical Japanese text on facing pages with the horizontal English text created gaps in both versions, with stanzas breaking across pages in ways that impacted readability. Also, the difference in text orientation made it impossible to compare the two versions side-by-side.

Fortunately, Japanese readers are also accustomed to reading horizontally, though not in books: contemporary Japanese business correspondence, advertising, and other documents use the same horizontal alignment as English. In an effort to present matching stanzas on facing pages in the bilingual edition, we decided to lay out the Japanese text horizontally.

Eric E. Hyett & Spencer Thurlow
Boston, MA and Kochi, Japan
December, 2015

TRANSLATORS' ACKNOWLEDGEMENTS

For permission to use material first printed by them, we owe thanks to the editors and publishers of *The Cincinnati Review* and *World Literature Today*.

Many thanks to Barbara Helfgott Hyett and the members of PoemWorks: The Workshop for Publishing Poets, who helped with every word of this book. Special thanks to Wendy Drexler, Pam Gemme, Shana Hill, Carol Hobbs, Alexis Ivy, Lori Kagan, Steven Nickman, Margaux Novak, Clara Silverstein, Connemara Wadsworth, Allen West, Margot Wizansky for wonderful edits, and a special note of deep appreciation to Grey Held for solving our issues with the stylistic *katakana*.

Thanks to Miyuki Yokota Nouguchi and Ryuji Nouguchi for connecting us with Ms. Minashita, and for fostering the development of this book. Also thanks to the students and staff at Hello School in Kochi, Japan for taking the time to field numerous questions.

Thanks to Sawako Nakayasu and Juliet Winters Carpenter for blazing the trail for us, and for taking an interest in our work.

AUTHOR BIOS

Kiriu Minashita was born in 1970 in Kanagawa Prefecture, Japan. She is a poet and sociologist, specializing in sociology of body culture. She received her doctorate and conducted additional post-doc studies at Waseda University School of Social Sciences in Tokyo. She currently lectures at Rikkyo University, Department of Sociology. Her first book of poems, "Sonic Peace" was published by Shichosha in 2005, and won the 11th annual Chuya Nakahara prize in 2006. Her second book, "The Z Border" (Shichosha, 2008) won the 49th annual Bansui Prize in 2008. Her critical writings include: "The Maddening Crowd: Hopes and Depression of the Deflation Generation" (Kobunsha New Books, 2009); "Rogue Women" (Aki Books, 2014), and "The Poverty Of The Single Mother" (Kobunsha New Books, 2014). She is the co-author of: "Womanhood 2.0" (NHK Publishing, 2013); "Why Do Mothers and Daughters Have Issues?" (NHK Publishing, 2014); "Men With No Place; Women With No Time" (Nikkei Publishing, 2014). She has also published, under her birth name Rieko Tanaka: "Notes on Happiness in the Heisei Era: Societal Transformation and 'The Stability Trap'" (Kobunsha New Books, 2011).

Eric E. Hyett lives in Brookline, MA, and works as a poet, copy writer and translator. He graduated from Harvard College in 1991 with a degree in Linguistics with Romance Languages, and a minor in Japanese. He also was a graduate fellow in MIT's Program in the History and Social Study of Science and Technology. Eric is a member of PoemWorks, the Workshop for Publishing Poets in Boston. His work has recently appeared in *The Cincinnati Review, The Hudson Review, Barrow Street, Antioch Review, Nimrod, Harvard Review Online*.

Spencer Thurlow is a poet and writer who grew up on the island of Martha's Vineyard, Massachusetts. He spent the past 3.5 years living in Kochi City, Japan translating poetry and working as an English teacher. His work has recently appeared in *The Worcester Review* and *The Comstock Review*, as well as *Pudding Magazine*. Prior publications include Lyrical Somerville. He graduated from Goucher College in 2010.